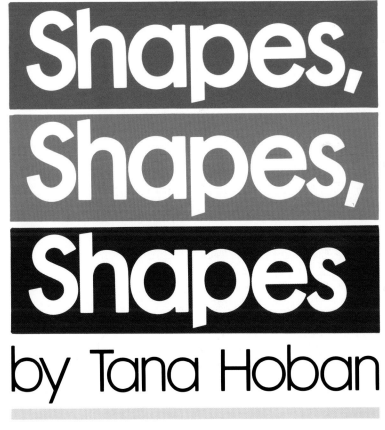

by Tana Hoban

Greenwillow Books  New York

Copyright © 1986
by Tana Hoban
All rights reserved.
No part of this book
may be reproduced or
utilized in any form
or by any means,
electronic or mechanical,
including photocopying,
recording or by any
information storage and
retrieval system,
without permission in writing
from the Publisher,
Greenwillow Books,
a division of
William Morrow &
Company, Inc.,
1350 Avenue of the Americas,
New York, NY 10019.
Printed in Hong Kong by
South China Printing Co.
First Edition
15 14 13 12 11 10 9 8 7

Library of Congress
Cataloging-in-Publication Data
Hoban, Tana.
Shapes, shapes, shapes.
Summary:
Photographs of familiar
objects such as chair,
barrettes, and manhole cover
present a study of
rounded and angular shapes.
1. Geometry—Juvenile literature.
[1. Shape—Pictorial works.
2. Geometry—Pictorial works]
I. Title.
QA447.H631986
516.2'15   85-17569
ISBN 0-688-05832-9
ISBN 0-688-05833-7 (lib. bdg.)

The photographs were reproduced
from 35-mm slides and printed in full color.
The typeface is Avant Garde.

for my mother

"And all that's best of dark and bright
Meet in her aspect and her eyes."—Lord Byron

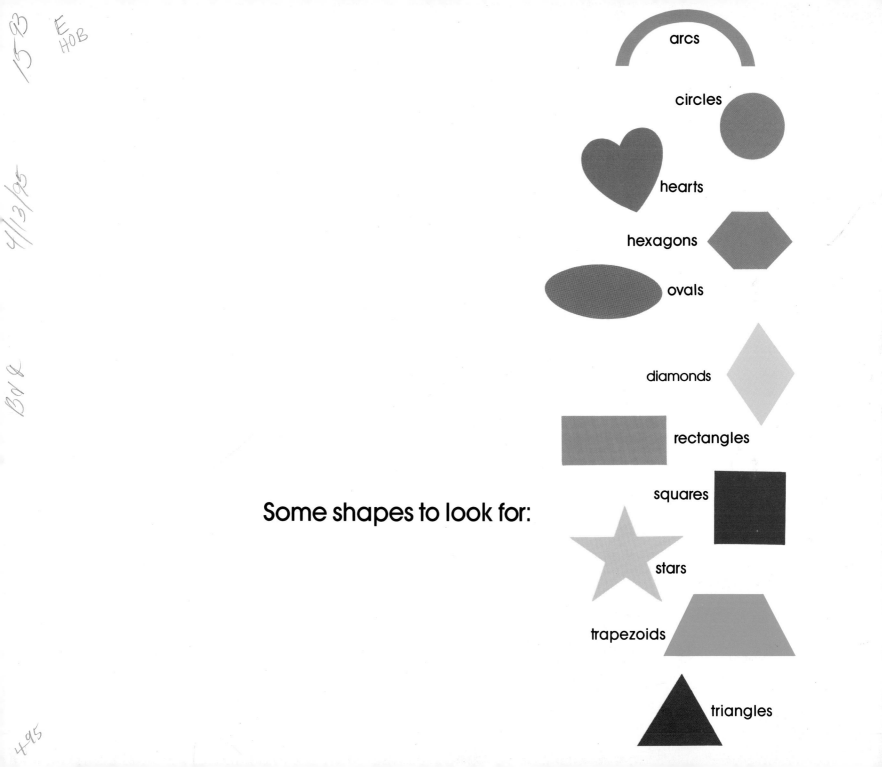

Some shapes to look for:

arcs

circles

hearts

hexagons

ovals

diamonds

rectangles

squares

stars

trapezoids

triangles

Shapes